THE MALFRED MURD COMIC FANTASY SERIES
BOOK CLUB COMPANION #1

CHAPTER-BY-CHAPTER CONVERSATION-STARTERS
FOR GROUPS READING
"FOOL'S PROOF" BY EVA SANDOR

BOOK CLUB COMPANION #1
Chapter-by-Chapter Conversation-starters
for groups reading FOOL'S PROOF.

Copyright © 2021, 2026. All rights reserved.
Cover illustration by Eva Sandor

Visit me at www.evasandor.com

AWKWARD SILENCE NO MORE!

So...you're reading the comical fantasy novel "Fool's Proof". No doubt you'll find plenty to ponder in the adventures of Malfred, Dame Elsebet, Corvinalias, and the other citizens of the as-yet-nameless Kingdom when they encounter surprising technology, dangerous doings, and what might be magic.

Spirited discussion is the heart of a book club, but if you aren't sure of your ability to come up with good questions on the fly— especially after the second Sherry Lorosso— fear not. This volume offers a shipload of suggestions to get your group bantering, blathering and having fun. Ask them as-is or make up your own variations. Let's go!

BEFORE YOU EVEN START READING...

- **What led your group to choose this book? Is comic fantasy a typical choice, or something new for you?**

- **From the very first page, you'll find that the author uses playful, complex and flamboyant language. What other books, stories or movies does it remind you of? Do you enjoy this kind of wordcraft, or does it stretch your comfort zone?**

- **The author is also an artist and drew the cover art. Do you think book covers are important? Why or why not?**

- **If you had the chance to ask the author a question, what might it be?**

Bonus: you can really do this! Just email me@evasandor.com

CHAPTER 1

In the first chapter, we're introduced to a literary world that is similar to our own— mostly. We meet our main character, see the kind of trouble he's found himself in, and leave him facing off with someone big and mean.

- **Does this setting remind you of a "real" historic time and place, or does it seem more like a fairy tale? If it's something in between, what would you call it?**

- **Malfred Murd (Fred) is clearly very talented, but still seems to rub people the wrong way. Do you find yourself liking or disliking Fred? Do you think readers need to like characters on a personal level in order to find them entertaining?**

- **Challenge each other to improvise a few good— and terrible!— poems.**

- **What is the most disgusting drink you've ever tasted?**

CHAPTER 2

This chapter takes us to quite another part of the Whellen Country: the home of its ruler, Dame Elsebet de Whellen, whose maids are preparing her for a feast.

- **What kind of person does Dame Elsebet seem to be? How does the author show her personality?**

- **The Whellen Country is the home of technologies more advanced than those of the rest of the Kingdom, and Whellengood Hall would probably fit in well among modern skyscrapers. Do you enjoy touches of anachronism in books and movies? Why or why not?**

- **Where would you draw the line between fantasy and science fiction?**

CHAPTER 3

Dame Elsebet hosts a grand feast to celebrate 50 years of her rule— but we learn that her family's title, and thus its claim to the Whellen Country, may be in jeopardy. She's made an ambitious plan to save it, but is consumed with worry over whether the plan is being carried out.

- **Dame Elsebet's brother refers to something upsetting in her past. What clues does the author give as to her backstory?**

- **Dame Elsebet considers it an ill omen that the messenger tasked with bringing her word of her plan's progress has not yet arrived. Do you believe in omens?**

- **Is the lightning strike another omen, or is Dame Elsebet reading too much into a natural phenomenon?**

CHAPTER 4

We get to know Alvert, the hapless messenger carrying news of Dame Elsebet's plan. He's had plenty of trouble with this job already— and finally, only a few miles from Whellengood Hall, the magpie Corvinalias steals the very important message that Dame Elsebet is waiting for.

- **The narration of Alvert's story is rendered in his own rustic dialect. What other books have you seen this technique used in? Do you enjoy reading the "sound" of language?**

- **For this book, the author researched the history of cursewords and invented a specific type of cursing for her characters to use. Where do you stand on the subject of bad language? Is it a creative outlet, a cultural phenomenon, or just plain rude?**

CHAPTER 5

Chasing Corvinalias, Alvert (literally) runs into the rich and beautiful shipping magnate Ata Maroo, the "Ox-Train Queen".

- The whole world seems to have hung a "kick me" sign on Alvert. The late, beloved TVTropes.org used to refer to this character type as a "chew toy" or "woobie". What other characters from books, movies, or media fit that description?

- Why do you think Ata Maroo would bother welcoming a nobody like Alvert into her business meeting?

- What techniques did the author use to evoke Alvert's progressing drunkenness?

CHAPTER 6

An irate barmaid chases Fred into an expensive inn, where he's recognized by his old acquaintance Ata Maroo. We learn some of Fred's backstory.

- Fred is clearly very much embittered by his past. What do you imagine his life was like as a young novice monk? Or in the Royal household?

- Do you find Fred to be a woobie also, or does something keep you from feeling sorry for him?

CHAPTER 7

Corvinalias brings Fred the stolen message bag, mistakenly thinking it is full of coins. Fred realizes it must belong to Dame Elsebet, and has the bright idea of taking it to her for a reward.

- **Do you get the feeling that this is the inciting incident, the match that lights the fuse of the story? What are some of your favorite inciting incidents from other books, movies and media?**

- **Does Corvinalias seem to be helpful to Fred, or a source of more trouble for him?**

CHAPTER 8

We meet Dame Elsebet's cousins the de Brewels, cheerfully self-absorbed rulers of their own vastly wealthy neighboring country. They learn that a lot of cash has just been stolen from their palace, but breathe a sigh of relief that thieves didn't get one of their priceless "spellbound" treasures.

- **What do you think of Dame Irona and Donn Felip? If you find them funny, can you explain why?**

- **The Grand Constable's investigation kicks off a crime subplot. Do you enjoy mysteries, police procedurals or other crime stories? Why or why not?**

- **Sometimes multiple genres mix in the same story. What do you think is the key to making this work? Where have you seen it done well— or badly?**

CHAPTER 9

Fred gets a ride to Whellengood Hall with Ata Maroo's wagon fleet— and is tormented by one of the ox-drovers along the way.

- **Ata Maroo has a big vocabulary, especially for terms related to her business, but she speaks with a definite foreign accent. Do you speak more than one language? Can you describe how you learned your second (or third, or fourth...) language, and when you use it?**

- **The ox-drover Nadima is a nasty piece of work— but it's played for laughs. How mean can characters get, and still be funny? What, for you, is going too far?**

CHAPTER 10

After the ill omen of the lightning strike, Dame Elsebet is convinced that her plan to save the Whellen Country has well and truly gone off the rails. After praying all night for some kind of help, she encounters Fred and mistakes him for a holy man, sent to her by the gods.

- **The first part of the chapter is written as if it were the thoughts of Dame Elsebet's horse. What other books have you seen this technique used in? Do you enjoy imagining animals' inner lives?**

- **What details made Dame Elsebet think Fred was the answer to her prayers? What made Fred think Dame Elsebet was a garden hermit? Have you ever misjudged someone because of first impressions?**

CHAPTER 11

In Coastwall, capital city of the Brewel Country, a fence makes a deal with a thief— a thief with a "spellbound" treasure to sell.

- What techniques does the author use to evoke a tense, unpleasant feeling?

- For this book, the author researched historic criminal slang, using some actual period terms and inventing others. Do you enjoy learning about words and their history? Does your family or circle of friends have a slang of its own?

CHAPTER 12

It dawns on Fred that the old peasant he's been trying to scam is Dame Elsebet herself— and she won't hesitate to execute him if she discovers he's a fraud. Before he can escape, the bag is opened, a secret is revealed, and Fred is roped into going on a quest.

- Dame Elsebet slew many monsters in her youth. Do you enjoy reading about mythical or fantastic creatures? What are some of your favorites?

- Nicolo, Dame Elsebet's head servant, seems to have sized Fred up as a con artist from the start. Why do you think Dame Elsebet would rather not listen to his warning?

- Could Fred have avoided all this, or did he bring it on himself? Do you think certain people just naturally find ways to get themselves into trouble and if so, what is it about them that causes it?

CHAPTER 13

Dame Elsebet's plan revolved around her protege, a healer known as Doktor Taluca Lively, who is also the world's only functional sorcerer. He was supposed to travel aboard a ship called the *Longwing*— but now we see the *Longwing* adrift, with its captain dead and those remaining aboard terrorized by a murderer run amok.

- **This chapter is extremely short, but intense. What techniques does the author use to evoke horror?**

- **Do you like scary stories? Why or why not? What are some of your favorites, or some that you found particuarly appalling?**

CHAPTER 14

Dame Elsebet and Fred take a mechanized carriage to a seemingly enchanted valley, there to try and do a piece of highly hazardous magic. With the help of Corvinalias, Fred pulls off an inspired piece of deception that makes her believe he really has powers.

- **The mechanized carriage is another example of the Whellen Country's high technology. Could you imagine what other fantasies or fairy tales might be like, if they included technological innovations?**

- **The Leet of the Heart was inspired by a real-life location. Have you ever been in the presence of a dangerous natural wonder and if so, what was it like?**

- **Fred tricks Dame Elsebet with a stage magic technique. Have you ever been fooled by a professional such as a magician, pickpocket or card sharp? Do you know any magic or psychological tricks of your own?**

CHAPTER 15

Dame Elsebet shows Fred the Heart of Stone, a massive natural waterwheel that provides the energy powering her country's Utopian economy.

- **Do you think the Heart of Stone is magic, or simply a freak of nature? How much does the genre of a book influence whether we see something as supernatural?**

- **How about the de Brewels' Twin Cans: do you think they're magical, or some kind of unexplained technology? Does it matter?**

- **Bonus: if anyone in your book club is a UW-Madison grad— try singing the Whellen Country anthem to the tune of "Varsity". (Recall that, in Chapter 3, Dame Elsebet's party guests waved their arms and swayed as they sang...)**

CHAPTER 16

Now aboard a mechanized riverboat, Dame Elsebet, Fred and Corvinalias continue their quest to find the lost Doktor Lively. Dame Elsebet reveals that she planned to present Doktor Lively to the King, as a bribe to sway his decision regarding the future of her country.

- **Fred desperately wants to avoid seeing the King again. What do you think happened between them back on the Isle of Gold? Or do you prefer not to speculate on a story as you read it?**

- **Dame Elsebet treats the fact that magpies have a civilization (and a nobility) as completely believable; also recall that Alvert was disgusted to have had his bag stolen by a "loud-mouthed braggin' magpie"— as if it's simply a given that they can speak to humans. Does that sort of detail make this book magical realism, low fantasy, absurdist fiction, or something else? Do such labels matter?**

CHAPTER 17

Alvert, fired for drunkenness and now working as a courier in Ata Maroo's wagon fleet, discovers he is head over heels for Ata Maroo— but has less than no idea what to do about it.

- **Being in love with someone unattainable is an evergreen fiction trope. Why do you think that is?**

- **Has it ever happened to you? Care to spill the details?**

CHAPTER 18

At the harbor in the city of Coastwall, the fence— who is revealed to be a powerful crime boss— now meets a crooked ship's captain. She forces him into smuggling the de Brewels' stolen treasure out of the Kingdom.

- **The powerful criminal was inspired by a real-life old lady crime boss in 19th-century New York City. Does discovering that a story has a basis in real life make you want to learn about history, or do you prefer to keep the worlds of fact and fiction separate?**

- **The ship's captain regrets that "but for circumstances, he might have had education". You've probably noticed that in the world of this book, manual labor is women's work— and that they do in fact seem to be larger and stronger than men. What implications would this have, if it were true in our world?**

CHAPTER 19

Back at Brewel Hall, Dame Irona and her husband discuss what little they know of Dame Elsebet's situation. Irona is still plagued by the thought that a criminal was among them.

- **What do you think of the de Brewels' wildly luxurious home? Do you think you could stay grounded in reality, if you lived in such surroundings?**

- **Dame Irona is clearly the type of featherbrained character meant to provoke laughter, with Donn Felip as her straight man. Why do you think this trope is so persistently popular?**

CHAPTER 20

After drinking up the contents of a certain bottle in a lovesick haze, Alvert gets lost and ends up in jail.

- **Have you ever become lost in a strange place?**

- **...after drinking the contents of a fancy crystal bottle?**

- **...that you were supposed to be bringing back to your charismatic billionaire boss?**

- **...who you are hopelessly in love with?**

    If you were able to answer "yes" to more than one of these questions: is your name, by any chance, Alvert Dragonsson?

CHAPTER 21

As the first port of call on their quest, Fred and Dame Elsebet arrive at her cousin Donn Felip's palatial home, Brewel Hall. Dame Elsebet thinks he will be able to help them, but she is prevented from seeing him until the morning.

- **The description of Brewel Hall continues to become even more outrageously lavish, reaching its height in a paragraph where the author stacks up a list of thirteen words describing the materials used in Fred's room— which, not surprisingly, provokes his claustrophobia. Do you like this style of wordplay? Or this style of decorating?**

- **Corvinalias is delighted to have "tamed" the de Brewels' pet, a cheetah-like creature known as a highcat. Have you ever had an encounter with a wild animal? What happened?**

CHAPTER 22

Donn Felip de Brewel's morning levee is interrupted first by his wife's interpretive dance performance, and then by the arrival of Dame Elsebet.

- **Dame Irona dances to orchestral music that the author describes in quite some detail. Were you able to "hear" it in your mind?**

- **If you found the dance funny, was it because you understood its symbolism— or because you didn't?**

- **Donn Felip seems used to such performances. Do you think he appreciates them, or just puts up with them? How would you react?**

CHAPTER 23

The de Brewels are no help at all to Dame Elsebet. But Fred, continuing his impersonation of a magical scholar/magician/monk, greatly impresses them— as well as their children, Petir and Kestrella.

- **What do you think Dame Irona almost said to Dame Elsebet— before she stopped herself?**

- **Did you like the poem Fred recited for Kestrella? What about her reaction to it?**

CHAPTER 24

Back in jail, Alvert finds Ata Maroo's two rich playboy lovers in the cell with him. Hilarity ensues, following which he is bailed out by Nadima, the same ox-drover who tormented Fred.

- **Did you find yourself rooting for Alvert? If so, was it because you've already identified him as a sympathetic character, or because you disliked the rich playboys? Or did you just sit back, with no judgment, and watch the slapstick unfold?**

- **Do you think we've seen the last of the playboys? Of Nadima?**

CHAPTER 25

Fred poses for Kestrella de Brewel in her hidden art studio, and has a sudden revelation: if he plays his cards right, he can escape from Dame Elsebet by staying with the de Brewels.

- **Do you think Kestrella was playing coy with her double entendres, or did Fred misunderstand them?**

- **The author, as mentioned before, is also a visual artist. Regarding her descriptions of Kestrella as she sketched Fred's portrait: do you think it's necessary to know how to do a thing, before you can write convincingly about it? Or do writers more often manage to fool us with superficial descriptions?**

CHAPTER 26

Nadima bails Alvert out of jail. But she doesn't take him back to work; instead, looking to make money, she tricks him into entering a prizefight by telling him the Champion wants to duel him for the hand of Ata Maroo.

- **The town crier makes it sound as though men's prizefighting is the Kingdom's up-and-coming sport, or at least very popular with gamblers. Are you a fan of anything with a passionate niche following? Do you go to great lengths to watch or take part in it?**

- **What do you think of Nadima's ability to turn on the charm when she needs to?**

- **What do you think will happen to Alvert? Or— as in a previous question— do you prefer not to speculate?**

CHAPTER 27

The de Brewels' luxurious self-indulgence is interrupted by a representative of the King, come to take away one of their "spellbound" objects as tribute. He chooses a pair of pewter tankards, which function as a kind of magical walkie-talkie. But before they can be revealed as fakes left by the thief, a fire breaks out.

- **The de Brewels seem to have no sense whatever that they are wasting Dame Elsebet's time. Do you think this is because they are disrespectful, or simply oblivious?**

- **Despite everything, do the de Brewels seem like a happy family? Do you think you'd like them?**

CHAPTER 28

In the panic, Dame Elsebet makes her escape from the tedious Brewel Hall, intent on continuing her search for Doktor Lively. Fred surprises himself by joining her in the little boat she rows across the river to the city of Coastwall, and earns the ire of Corvinalias, who takes his leave of Fred forever.

- **The symbolism of Dame Elsebet's faded, forgotten wedding tattoos is obvious to Fred, though he doesn't want to ask for details. How do you think her husband might have died?**

- **Corvinalias wants to stay at Brewel Hall, reminding Fred that he himself had planned never to return to the royal Isle of Gold. But Fred is clearly experiencing some kind of mixed feelings— why do you think this might be?**

CHAPTER 29

Ata Maroo is annoyed with Nadima for stealing things from her— including Alvert. Now we discover why she cares about the "stupid man": he resembles the god of her people.

- **Ata Maroo berates herself, saying she ought to forget her homeland. Do you think you can command yourself to forget something, or is that like trying not to think of a pink elephant?**

- **The religion of the Peaceful Ocean is extremely simple. Do you think anyone in our world would follow it?**

CHAPTER 30

Dame Elsebet and Fred, pursuing their own investigation into the disappearance of Doktor Lively, find their way to the Coastwall Station House, but learn that the Grand Constable cannot help them.

- **Dame Elsebet has a prodigiously good memory for directions. Do you? Or are you more the type who could get lost a block from home?**

- **Dame Elsebet mentions having been "quite daring" in her youth. What kind of upbringing do you think she had?**

CHAPTER 31

Ata Maroo confronts her past and with a huge emotional effort, decides she must give up her successful life in the Kingdom and return to her old home to take up a duty she's been neglecting.

- **Were you surprised at Ata Maroo's eloquence, when she spoke in her native language? Why or why not?**

- **Do you agree with the speech made by Ata Maroo's "voice of duty, which was her own voice"? Does it remind you of any philosophies, ancient or modern, espoused by people in our own world?**

CHAPTER 32

A long night of investigation bears fruit, as Dame Elsebet and Fred discover what happened to the *Longwing*: it was hijacked.

- **What details tip us off that Fred is starting to identify with Dame Elsebet, despite telling himself he plans to escape from her?**

- **The sailor who tells Dame Elsebet about the <u>Longwing</u> has "a very entertaining way about him". Have you ever met someone who could make even the most boring story interesting? What do you think is such a person's secret?**

CHAPTER 33

Ata Maroo wishes to protect her parents from the burden of choosing her a new husband. Her first playboy is too spoiled and greedy; she sends him on his way. The second one takes her to a popular entertainment— the men's prizefight— but he turns out to be too vain and arrogant. She spurns him as well, but then spots the treacherous Nadima with her stolen pawn Alvert.

Alvert is spectacularly beaten in the prizefight. Ata Maroo deals summarily with Nadima, then takes pity upon Alvert and brings him to her wagon.

- **"Everything repeats itself" - "No note ever sounds, without some note in echo". Besides the echo/repeat in this chapter— Alvert and the aurochs calf— what other events in the book have you noticed that mirror one another, or are variations on the same theme? Do you notice this happening in real life?**

CHAPTER 34

Aboard the *Longwing*, the villain is revealed to be not only a murderer, but a psychotic—and possibly magical— torturer, whose last living victim now draws near a fate worse than death.

- **The author is not usually a fan of the macabre; for this project, she took care to teach herself by studying some very frightening and gruesome short stories, including the classic <u>Lost Face</u> by Jack London. Do you have a favorite horror writer? What techniques do you think work really well?**

CHAPTER 35

Using the very skills that let her save the abandoned aurochs calf with the broken foot, Ata Maroo cares for Alvert. He passes the moral tests the playboys failed and it's clear to her that, despite his lowly position, he is everything she needs in a husband.

- **Did you see this coming? If you did, were you looking forward to it? If it was a surprise, is it a pleasant one?**

- **With 97 pages still left in the book, Ata Maroo and Alvert clearly still have things to do together. What do you hope will happen to them?**

CHAPTER 36

In Coastwall Harbor, Dame Elsebet seeks someone to take her out into the Midland Sea and hunt for Doktor Lively. The crooked smugglers' ship is the only one that agrees; its captain, miserable at having to bend the knee to his new shipowner the crime boss, sees an opportunity to hold Dame Elsebet for ransom.

- **Despite his self-proclaimed wish to escape from Dame Elsebet, Fred remains at her side, looking out for her wellbeing in ways such as advice on dealing with the captain. Do you think he even realizes what he's doing?**

- **Does the ship's captain seem savvy enough to deal with the crime boss? How about his crew: do they strike you as being behind him all the way?**

CHAPTER 37

At a posh hotel in Coastwall, Ata Maroo prepares to sell her business empire and her husband experiences his first taste of luxury...

- **What is it that feels so good about scenes where downtrodden characters are finally treated well?**

- **Can you think of other scenes from books, movies and media where this happens? What are some of your favorites?**

- **Do you think Ata Maroo loves Alvert back, or is theirs strictly a marriage of convenience?**

CHAPTER 38

...and meanwhile, in another room at the same hotel, Fred makes plans to give Dame Elsebet the slip and head back to Brewel Hall, there to live life as the world's fanciest garden hermit and never, ever again think about the Isle of Gold or the life he'd once had there.

- **Although he has been knocked about of late, in contrast with Alvert Fred is familiar with luxury. Is it as much fun seeing him get the room, the food, the clothes and the pampering? Why or why not?**

- **The author has Fred look into a mirror— but she doesn't use this age-old cliché to tell us very much about his looks. His state of wear and tear are described, but not his features— in fact, at the opening of Chapter 1, we're told Fred has "a face so unexceptional the guard really couldn't have described it". So: what do you think he looks like?**

    (Even the author admits she doesn't really know! Sure, she drew the cartoon covers—but they're more about attitude than literal appearance.)

CHAPTER 39

Corvinalias went back to Brewel Hall, expecting his delight at taming the highcat to continue; instead, he became bored with life there. In search of new adventure, he reaches the hotel and— attracted by the mass of coins in Ata Maroo's suite— decides to make Alvert his new pet.

- **Did you enjoy the description of Corvinalias's flight across the city? Did you notice the musical or poetic techniques the author used?**

- **Corvinalias almost doesn't recognize Alvert. Have you ever failed to recognize someone, because they were out of context?**

CHAPTER 40

If you haven't read the book yet, be careful! This chapter contains a twist!

- Well, well, well! Discuss.

- What other literary twists have you enjoyed? Hated? Been surprised by? Managed to guess ahead of time?

CHAPTER 41

Fred joins Dame Elsebet for one final meal, but finds himself tormented by the nameless feeling that's been plaguing him since the very start of the book. With the entrance of Ata Maroo his deception is finally, and spectacularly, revealed— and his confrontation with Dame Elsebet is explosive, causing him to face a truth he has long tried to hide from himself.

Afterward, determined to return to the royal Isle of Gold, Fred stows away on the only vessel bound there: the same ship Dame Elsebet plans to take. And, in his hiding place aboard, he discovers something...

- Were you surprised at Dame Elsebet's backstory, or had you suspected something like it?

- Even if you thought Fred was a jerk up until now, did you feel for him when "something inside him burst"? Or will it take still more to give you a change of heart?

- In his hiding place in the locker of the dinghy, Fred finds the smugglers' cache, holding the spellbound tankards stolen from the de Brewels— and into them he "whispers the words he longs to hear". The author leaves these a mystery, like Bill Murray's closing words in <u>Lost in Translation</u>. What do you think they are?

CHAPTER 42

With the convenient help of arson in the harbor, the smugglers' ship manages to run the blockade and escape out into the Midland Sea.

- **It's becoming obvious that the captain is <u>not</u> savvy enough to deal with his new shipowner, the crime boss. How do you imagine this trip will go for him?**

CHAPTER 43

Aboard the drifting *Longwing,* The villain shows us his demented rage.

- **What techniques does the author use to bring readers into the mind of the villain?**

- **The deranged villain is a very common trope— did the author manage to make this man, and his mental state, seem fresh and vivid to you? Why or why not?**

CHAPTER 44

Aboard the smugglers' ship, the captain attempts to take Dame Elsebet prisoner, hoping to extort a ransom from someone back in the Whellen Country. He goes so far as to threaten her life—wrong decision.

- **If you expected the captain to meet a bad end: who did you think would cause it?**

- **The weaponized fan is nothing new— but did you see it coming? In what other books, movies or media have you seen a similar weapon?**

- **Easter egg! Do you recognize Dame Elsebet's line, "there's been a dreadful accident"?**

CHAPTER 45

Corvinalias starts questioning his decision to sail for the Peaceful Ocean with Alvert and Ata Maroo: it seems boring. That is, until he finds a pod of Cloud Whales— which go rushing off toward Ata Maroo's boat.

- **Have you ever assumed you'd be bored with something, only to find that it was actually far more interesting, or exciting, than you thought it would be? Can you share the story?**

- **Why do you think the whales want to find Ata Maroo?**

CHAPTER 46

Although the captain isn't much missed, Dame Elsebet is discovered to be a valuable quantity and the rest of the sailors attack her. She proves more than capable of fighting them off, but Fred panics, comes out of hiding and is captured.

The whales turn out to be Ata Maroo's onetime driving team and their calves. In his zeal to go find more such wonders, Corvinalias spots the fracas aboard the smuggling ship— and Fred, in danger.

- **Do you think Fred should have controlled himself and stayed hidden in the dinghy, or was it his duty to come to Dame Elsebet's assistance?**

- **Back home in her country, Ata Maroo's family ran a shipping business—driving whales instead of oxen, towing huge boats instead of wagons. Does her success as the "Ox-Train Queen" seem easier to understand, in light of this?**

CHAPTER 47

The whales rescue Fred and Dame Elsebet by capsizing the smugglers' ship.

- **Fun speculation: could real-life whales, if sufficiently angry and determined, really turn a ship upside down? How big would they, or the ship, have to be?**

CHAPTER 48

Two stories of the villain's past: one, the front he presented to an unwitting patron. Two, the truth.

- **In this chapter, the narration makes a drastic shift as it addresses the matter of the villain's origin; it shifts still further as it drills down into the truth.**

  Did you notice the mechanics of the technique— for instance, how the second story is written in the present tense— or only the mood? What effect did it have on you? Do you think this was a good choice on the author's part, or would you have presented this information in some other way?

CHAPTER 49

All the characters are together aboard Ata Maroo's catamaran when they spot the drifting *Longwing*. Only Fred senses something is amiss, but he is persona non grata; he pushes his warnings just a bit too far and evokes the rage of Dame Elsebet.

- **By now, Fred has identified the sick feeling he'd been having as guilt: Guilt, for mistreating the King— a troubled boy his own age who he'd been brought to the royal Isle as a companion for. Does this revelation of Fred's backstory seem surprising, or sadly inevitable?**

- **Earlier in the book, we discovered that Fred has a knack for discerning trickery— and he spots the villain as a liar, although**

he cannot explain why, beyond "takes one to know one".
Do you think that's it? In what ways are Fred and the villain similar?

- **Do you believe Dame Elsebet this time?**
  If she sees Fred again, will she really execute him?

CHAPTER 50

In this chapter, we shift to the villain's viewpoint and hear his *cri de coeur* about being troubled with some terrible impotence of will— a feeling he cannot recognize as compassion.

- **Certain literature on psychopathy asserts that psychopaths' lack of empathy means they cannot experience guilt.**

  According to this model guilt, being born of the need to confess wrongdoing, requires another person to confess to— and to psychopaths, others are not really people at all; the very notion of guilt is, therefore, incomprehensible.

  However, they can and do feel shame instead. This is because shame is much more primitive, born only of the need to hide one's weaknesses. Do you agree with this model? What light does it shed on the difference between Fred and the villain?

CHAPTER 51

More from the villain. Now he and his patron, Dame Elsebet, are on the Isle of Gold. With one final burst of effort, the villain overcomes his "flaw" of compassion and heads for the royal palace.

- **Now that his only speck of compassion is gone, the villain is more dangerous than ever. What do you think he's planning?**

- **Did you find yourself experiencing the villain's twisted and corrupt mental state along with him? What techniques did the author use to evoke it?**

CHAPTER 52

Fred has landed on the Isle of Gold himself. He arrives at the royal palace to find it hauntingly empty. Something is very wrong…

- **If the King were alive here and now, his form of mental dysfunction would have a proper diagnosis. Do you think people of this time and place understood it? Was finding the young King a companion a good idea?**

- **Did you find the Queen to be an interesting character? Is she a good match for the King?**

- **Did Fred's solution, and his heroism, surprise you? Why or why not?**

CHAPTER 53

The royal family is saved. Fred awakes from ther fever/coma that followed his wound, and is rewarded with a "boon": his choice of anything that is within the King's power to give.

- **What do you think he should ask for?**

- **What would you ask for?**

CHAPTER 54

Our story reaches its end. Fred and Dame Elsebet share a tense moment but reconcile. Fred reveals that the boon he asked for was for the de Whellens to be granted their title in perpetuity, so as never to lose their beloved country.

- **What emotions did you feel at the ending, and what techniques did the author use to evoke them?**

IN CONCLUSION...

You've reached the end of a journey with the characters of "Fool's Proof". Now it's time to talk about the book as a whole—at least, until you begin reading the rest of the series!

- Regarding the title: to "prove" something can mean to put it to the test. What kind of test was Fred put to? Were any of the other characters tested? Did they pass or fail?

- Which moments in the book did you think were funniest? Most exciting? Most touching? Or were there parts you would change, if it were up to you?

- Which characters were your favorites? Was it because you liked them— or because you enjoyed disliking them?

- If you were making a movie of this book, which actors would you cast? Or would it be an animated movie? What kind of soundtrack do you imagine it having?

- Bonus: The villain's name contains a secret. Do anagrams with its letters until you (actually...) unlock it!

We hope you'll keep reading the rest of *The Malfred Murd Comic Fantasy Series!* Look for the sequels at your favorite online retailer. Sales links at:

www.books2read.com/evasandor

NOTES

NOTES

If your book club enjoyed discussing "Fool's Proof",
please leave it a rating or review it on
Amazon, Goodreads or your other favorite sites.

You can also sign up for the author's newsletter at

evasandor.com